Clara Elizabeth Choate

Songs of Truth

Clara Elizabeth Choate

Songs of Truth

ISBN/EAN: 9783743303744

Manufactured in Europe, USA, Canada, Australia, Japa

Cover: Foto ©Thomas Meinert / pixelio.de

Manufactured and distributed by brebook publishing software
(www.brebook.com)

Clara Elizabeth Choate

Songs of Truth

BY

CLARA ELIZABETH CHOATE

AUTHOR OF MODERN SCIENCE OF BODY

SECOND EDITION

LEE AND SHEPARD PUBLISHERS

10 MILK STREET

BOSTON

"A verse will find him
Whom a sermon flies."

Contents

My Pearls

THESE are my pearls,
  Gathered on the highway
Of life's immortal thought;
  Precious jewels in the pathway,
Like angel message brought.
  These are my pearls.

Forever

Love is the grandest truth of life,
  Forever, oh, forever.
Love toils for duty without strife,
  And wearies never, never.
Love is the sunshine for all tears,
Love is the strength o'er all the fears,
Love is the goal of all the years,
  Forever, oh, forever.

Love is the harmony of the soul,
  Forever, oh, forever.
Love is the great and wondrous whole,
  And changes never, never.
Love is the heaven earth will find,
Love is the spirit of mankind,
Love is the triumph truth will bind,
  Forever, yes, forever.

Life's Work

It matters not so very much
  Where the great work of life begins,
If only love shall lead the way,
  Since love's grand law forever wins.

To follow up the high desire,
  Nor falter by the wayside lone,
For truth's conviction guides aright,
  Divinest gift true souls must own.

The falsities of earthly hopes
  May ever tempt and plead their claim,
But steadfast purpose disinthralls,
  And faith's pure light makes all things plain.

Truth's royalty will clothe with power
  The soul's sublime ideal;
Earth will defend and heaven will guard
  Love's mightiest guest, the real.

Firm trust and patience oft renew
　　Their vigil watch for truth and right;
That life's immortal work may move
　　In love's full measure of God's light.

True love must underlie all work,
　　Must override all doubt and fear ;
Life's inspiration must be truth,
　　Life's conquest gained when love is near.

My Appeal

Come listen to the words of Christ,
  Whose truth is peace and health,
Unfold thy heart to things divine,
  Whose gifts are greatest wealth.

Bow down thine ear to love's sweet strain,
  Sung through the life of Him
Whose glory shines in lifting up
  From sickness, weakness, sin.

No thought He gave to humankind
  But thrills the world to-day ;
Love's law the heavens must emulate,
  Love's law man must obey.

For thee His blessings freely wait,
　His faith, His truth, His might;
So lay aside earth's doubts and fears,
　Receive His wondrous light.

No measure unto thee is given ;
　Seek though thy strength is tried ;
Make Christ thine own, thyself a Christ,
　Then shalt thou be satisfied.

Love

Living in the sunlight forever
  Of love, is the crowning of life ;
'Tis the hope human hearts sweetly cherish
  Mid the seeming of weakness and strife.

And the fulness of love's joyful birthright
  Beams clear on the vision of man,
Revealing the highest conception
  Of spirit, and God's wondrous plan.

For goodness chases the shadows
  Called sickness and sorrow and sin,
Beyond the hills of earth's morning,
  Till love's glory and splendor shine in.

Transforming the earth into heaven,
  Translating the human and weak,
Till love alone is the living,
  And love only the words men speak.

For love is the soul and redeemer,
  And love is the Christ men must find ;
And love, pure love, is the saviour,
  Life's helper, and health of mankind.

Retrospection

WHAT would I have,
   Of all that could· be given,
To make my life more sweet,
   A truer song from heaven,

If fortune, friends, and fame
   Were easy prey to win,
And every joy of earth
   Like magic could float in?

What would I seek,
   More eager to possess,
Than poet's genius of the soul,
   True touch of holiness?

What would I know
   Of life, humane, divine,
E'en though the mystery of death
   Dissolved by thought of mine?

'Tis surely this,
    The truth, the life, the way,
That perfect spirit of the Christ,
    Whose light makes endless day.

His power sublime
    To comfort, heal, and bless,
My own must be, if work
    Will bring such worthiness.

This Christ-like love,
    My own, thy own, can be,
'Tis life's immortal hope,
    And crowns eternity.

Speak The Word Only

SPEAK the word only, its presence is health,
    Unto all people, 'tis life, love, and wealth ;
Breathe it so grandly, other voices are still,
    Silenced is evil, the word is God's will.

Speak the word only, speak without fear,
    Till the dumb too shall speak, and the deaf they
        shall hear ;
Speak it so plainly, the lame leap for joy,
    That the bondage of sin its truths may destroy.

Speak the word only, in magic or rhyme,
    Simple its language, its tone is sublime ;
For the word is God's truth, its balm, and its might,
    Is the healing of nations, the triumph of right.

Speak the word only, with spirit and power
  Of the soul's deep conviction, born of the hour
When the light of the word fills the heart with the
    love
  Of manhood's divinity, the Christ from above.

Speak the word only, till all night is done,
  Till day shines forever, heaven's glory is won,
And all nations in truth and in spirit shall see
  Man's oneness with God, the word that makes free.

Beneficence

Only a word so kindly given,
    What then?
Only a look this side of heaven,
    Just when
The heart with lingering sigh
    And tear,
Entering that city strange,
    Did hear
A voice so strongly sweet,
In tones of love complete,
And words so fitly meet
    With sympathy.

Only a touch of tender hands
    So true,
Only a graceful smile in lands
    So new;
There in the far-off scene
    Of light,

Filling the day most sweet
    And bright,
A face did so impress,
Its kindliness did so caress,
Nor time nor distance can repress
    Love's memory.

Trifles only on the highway
    So great,
Seeming incidentals in the by-play
    Of fate ;
Dream was never known more fair
    Nor sure,
Never was kindness seen more rare
    Or pure,
Never could soul more richly feed
With measure full of heaven's meed,
Or give more love for human need :
    Love is divine.

My Petition

LIFT me up, O heavenly Father,
  Till I feel thy strength sublime;
Let thy spirit be my spirit,
  Let me have no will but Thine.

Bring into my life, O Father,
  Just the music of thy soul;
May the radiance of thy power
  All my words and deeds control.

Wake within my heart, O Giver
  Of divinest good and gain,
A response forever quickening
  Into action love's refrain.

Open wide of thy hid treasure,
  Priceless more than pearl of sea;
Meet my earnest, soulful longing
  For thy truth, — earth's mystery.

Fill my soul with revelation
  Yet awaiting humankind,
Teach me of thy boundless loving,
  How the Christ all men may find.

Breathe through me thine own perfection,
  Till my heart no more shall see
Aught but thy divine expressing
  Of love's grand eternity.

Down by the Sea

THAT was a beautiful day, O friend,
    Down by the sea,
When the wind's whispering brought love in its trend
    For you and me.
Then my heart rose from its sorrow and woes,
    Blessing the day,
That its sunlight had given a foretaste of heaven
    On earth's highway.

That was a glorious night, O love,
    And stars looked down,
While a sweetness reigned with the silence above,
    Like the hills' dark frown.
And with faltering sigh life's pleasures go by —
    A farewell is said.
For shadows will come, and souls must grow dumb
    When love's light has fled.

But a morning will come so fair, my own,
      When we shall meet,
Heaven's portal be gained, the darkness o'erthrown,
      Joy at our feet.
While the splendor of love will shine from above
      In gladness free,
Filling day and the night with love's morning bright,
      Down by the sea.

Light

Oh, the Light! Immortal radiance,
　Flung across life's stormy wave,
Burdened souls will feel thy cadence,
　Hearts distressed thy love will save.

Oh, the Light! Divine forever,
　Blessings rich thy ways unfold;
Grandest hope of man has never
　Compassed all thy truth untold.

Oh, the Light! Thy brightness beaming
　Rescues man from every fear;
Gone the shadows and the seeming;
　Light of day comes full and clear.

Oh, the Light! Supreme, eternal,
　Waking human hearts to see
Thine own goodness reigns supernal;
　Changeless bonds link them to Thee.

Truth

Out of a golden silence
   Comes ever a voice of love,
Bringing us thoughts of heaven
   And the angel life above.

And the tones so full of sweetness,
   Make memory still more dear,
Picturing forms and faces
   Of the lost who yet are near.

For death is only a curtain
   Hiding our loved ones from sight,
Which truth and science will open,
   Revealing God's way as right.

And right is forever spirit,
   The life of love bestowed,
Is the music sweet of angels,
   The sunshine of man's abode.

My Message

O CHILDREN of earth, God is speaking
  In the music of love's power divine,
His spirit, the eternal unfolding,
  Chant's the measure of life's song sublime.

To the hungry, oppressed, and faint-hearted
  His truth he pours out full and free ;
His bounty and mercy are endless
  As the white sands tossed back by the sea.

Neither wish, tear, nor sigh is unnoticed ;
  O children of earth, do you hear ?
Not a pulse-beat of joy or of anguish,
  But finds answer when love is so near.

O hearts, bowed down and so wearied !
  O eyes, oft filled with sad tears,
And with longings forever unuttered !
  O souls, burdened ever with fears !

O dreamers of pain and of pleasures!
O champions of right over wrong!
Love's law is ever the conqueror,
Love's music the only true song.

Listen then in the stillness of spirit,
All good is thine own, truth will say;
Its love-tone thy life will enrapture,
Till the shadows of earth fade away.

Rejoice, be glad, in the freedom of truth!
Rise, live, in the strength of God's will!
The might of the Christ is ever thine own,
Every need of thy soul Christ can fill.

Consolation

A HUSH is over the house,
  And a silence reigns supreme,
For the presence of one beloved
  Is gone like a bright day dream.

To join the great forever
  Is the joyous soul now flown,
Into the realm of eternal life,
  Where spirit shall know its own.

Vacant the place, no greeting
  For the loved ones left in sorrow ;
Narrower grows the circle here,
  Less planning for earth's to-morrow.

Hearts wrung with anguish still bless
  The dear one whose earth-work is done.
Ah! life seems of sadness so full,
  So rough seems the pathway to run.

And yet above all there is comfort,
　　Christ leading revealeth the way,
True faith illumines the darkness,
　　And God's love turns night into day.

Lo! the silence of death seems the counting
　　Twixt the measure of life's grand whole.
Life is God — his song, man immortal;
　　Each note is a deathless soul.

Work

—

On, the glory of occupation!
  Oh, the blessing of work well done!
Honest toil is the pride of creation,
  There is nothing nobler under the sun.

Grimy faces, with souls pure and holy,
  Hard, rough hands, with a purpose strong,
Shoulders bent, bearing earth's burden lowly —
  Fitting theme for heaven's own song.

Not more sweet is love than labor,
  Not more true is its mission grand,
Worth enthrones, and with heaven's favor
  Crowned is work; it is God's command.

Oh, the glory of occupation!
  Oh, the blessing of work well done!
Honest toil is the pride of creation,
  There is nothing nobler under the sun.

Recognition

I WALK no more alone,
  Unseen my God is near;
Divinely sweet, this love unknown,
  Trust is sublime, faith knows no fear.

I walk no more alone,
  Thy light dawns full and free,
The soul's deep echoes nearer home
  Wake fullest consciousness of thee.

I walk no more alone,
  Thou art forever here
With me, whose life no more can roam —
  Love's true content can bring no tear.

I walk no more alone,
   The head, the heart, the feet,
Touched by the spirit's finest tone,
   Move to thy measure, full, complete.

I walk no more alone,
   The whole of love is mine ;
No power of earth from dust to throne
   Can separate my life from Thine.

The Heart

Deep down against my heart
  So many lean, so many,
Scarce can I think how to impart
  The needed strength to any.

Yet still a faith comes ever near,
  I shall be more than ready
To ease their burdens, lessen fear,
  While love will hold me steady.

Our hearts are greater than we know,
  And love is never ending,
As truth, eternal truth, must show,
  'Tis life's great glory sending.

And hearts grow really strong,
    By calls to highest duty,
Their work can weave no wrong,
    When filled with love's own beauty.

For hearts in purest light
    Shine in the heart's best giving ;
Trust brings the power of sight,
    And love is truest living.

Trust

Sometimes the heart grows weary
　　Battling against earth's wrong,
Sometimes the feet will falter,
　　Though duty calls be strong.
Sometimes the eye looks downward,
　　And hope seems almost fled,
While watcher and waiter can only pray
　　For light, when truth seems dead.

Yet amid the seeming and doubting,
　　Amid all the wrong and the fear,
Stands forever the love of the Father,
　　Shines the light of His countenance clear.
For, born of His spirit, men conquer,
　　And, born of His love, men win ;
His truth is the anthem of triumph,
　　His strength is the victory o'er sin.

Truth, won by faith, is life's glory,
  And the triumph, 'mid doubt and despair,
Crowns with power the eternal unfolding
  Of the heights and the depths of God's care.
Till the soul in its glorious freedom
  Transposes all power as divine,
Finding rest in the infinite oneness,
  And on earth finding life is sublime.

Nature's Song and Story

The flowers in the grasses are singing,
  Earth hears not the song;
In the tree-tops an anthem is ringing,
  Birds sweetly the notes prolong.

The rocks under foot are repeating
  The cry of the stars unheard,
With the winds and the seas ever beating
  A chorus in unknown word.

While the sunshine filled with the splendor
  Of that beautiful myst'ry life,
Ever deep in the heart is the wonder
  At the very absence of strife.

Could the human but hear nature's story,
  Told by the flower, star, or stone,
And their wonderful love-songs of glory,
  He would make them ever his own.

An Answer

I HAVE read thy poem tender
  Of gray eyes' soft light,
And of snowy christening glory,
  Crown of hair so white;

And thy lines in sweetest music
  Tuned the air and sea,
Till the earth seemed only harp-strings,
  Whispering love to thee.

Just the flowing, silvery cadence
  Of love's song divine;
Just the burst in soul uplifting
  Of love's thought sublime;

Rippling melody of heart-chimes,
  Given by love unseen,
Pulses sweet of soul unbounded,
  Hope waves of a dream.

Faithful is love's gentle memory,
  Weaving holy strain,
Brighter earth for such pure singing ;
  Seeming loss is gain.

And the sea of stars give answer,
  I, thy love, am free,
But my freedom binds me closer,
  Closer, love, to thee.

And the same deep, wondrous love-link,
  Wide as crystal sea,
Will gather in the longshore line,
  And bring thy love to thee.

Love's Will

O UNIVERSE, so grand!
The whole great world expand
    In tenderness ;
Born of thy strength divine,
Caught up in strains sublime,
    Of holiness.
Thy soul's deep heart-desire
Fills human need with fire,
    Love's clearest light ;
Lifting earth's care-worn child,
Through Thy truth all undefiled,
    In radiance bright ;
Till woe and sorrow cease,
That cry for unknown peace,
    Is hushed and still,
And Christ's own healing power,
Like clouds of joy in shower —
    This is love's will.

A Memory

'Twas a day to be remembered
  When we climbed that mountain height,
When Corcovado in grandeur
  With Tijuca rose in sight ;
Sister ranges robed in splendor,
  Peaks few rival mountains know,
There, amid the southern breezes,
  Where Janeiro's mild winds blow.

Air and earth were heavy laden
  With the fruits' own rich perfume,
And the rising sun rays melted
  Into dreams of golden tune.
Subtle as the Eden glories
  Stole their beauty o'er our soul,
While with gentle lope the horses
  Bore us onward to our goal.

Baffled is all speech in telling
  Of the varied landscape glow;
Baffled is all thought and feeling
  As we gaze on scenes below;
Silenced, deep in meditation,
  Leave we all our world behind,
As if rising higher compelled us
  More to reverence nature's kind.

Still we journey on and upward,
  When, behold, I am alone,
Comes no answer to my shouting
  Save the echoes of my own.
Visions wild of mangled horseman —
  Terror filled both heart and brain;
Quickly I retraced the pathway,
  Round steep curves my horse did rein.

There to find my fears outwitted
  By the steed who fell behind,
All undaunted pressed we forward,
  With uplifted heart and mind.
Horse and man took friendly parting,
  For the roadway fast grew steep,
Still Tijuca's rocky summit
  Seemed stretched into vaulted deep.

High and grim in stern defiance
　　Towered the battling walls above,
But not stronger than our courage,
　　And not grander than our love.
Grasped we firm those chains of iron
　　Niched into that rocky side,
Till, appalled, we stood triumphant,
　　Trembling, weak, from very pride.

There protected from the sun rays,
　　Under bush, and brake, and fern,
Dreamed we of old Rio's offing,
　　Dreamed of love and our return.
All too soon our dream was over,
　　And the swing of spreading sail
Beckoned, till our faltering footsteps
　　Bore us down midst heaven's veil.

Oh, the memory is entrancing,
　　Heaven itself seems resting there;
Nor can future hold more splendor,
　　Nor dream visions be more fair.
Even though life is wrapt in sorrow,
　　Veiled in clouds of saddest pain,
Yet Tijuca's mountain glory
　　Speaks love's paradise again.

A Stray Thought

If we follow the right God's way we shall see,
   From day unto day in the guidance of heaven;
If we live near his love our worship will be
   A trust so divine, and all else that is given
But unites man to God, a bond never riven,
    And the truth that sets free.